SCULPTING GNOMES FOR BEGINNERS

The Ultimate Guide on How to Carve and Sculpt Amazing Gnomes Projects

Boris Joseph

Copyright@2021

TABLE OF CONTENT

CHAPTER 1 3

   INTRODUCTION 3

CHAPTER 2 5

   MATERIALS AND TOOLS TO SCULPT GNOMES 5

CHAPTER 3 8

   STEP BY STEP TO SCULPT GNOMES 8

CHAPTER 4 44

   HOW TO CARVE GNOMES WITH WOOD 44

THE END 56

CHAPTER 1

INTRODUCTION

Everybody enjoys a good gnome, but why settle for someone else's interpretation of what a gnome might be doing in your yard when you can create your own interpretation?

Anyone can construct a gnome out of polymer clay, and this guide will show you how. It doesn't require any complicated techniques or specialized materials, so anyone can do it :)

Let's get this party started.....

CHAPTER 2

MATERIALS AND TOOLS TO SCULPT GNOMES

Materials

Polymer clay covering around half of one of the large chunks (I should note that you could do this guide with multiple colours of clay to make the skin, clothes etc but I am doing it this way as its a bit cheaper).

Arcylic paint is a kind of paint.

Tin foil is a kind of aluminum foil.

Varnish.

For smoothing things out, wet wipes or a tub of water will suffice.

Tools

Sculpting tools are used in this process. You may use toothpicks and paper clips for this; you don't need any specialized equipment.

Knife for crafting.

Paintbrushes are used for painting.

Oven.

A rolling pin or a glass bottle, which may be used to roll out clay, is also useful, but not required.

CHAPTER 3

STEP BY STEP TO SCULPT GNOMES

Step 1: Getting Things Started

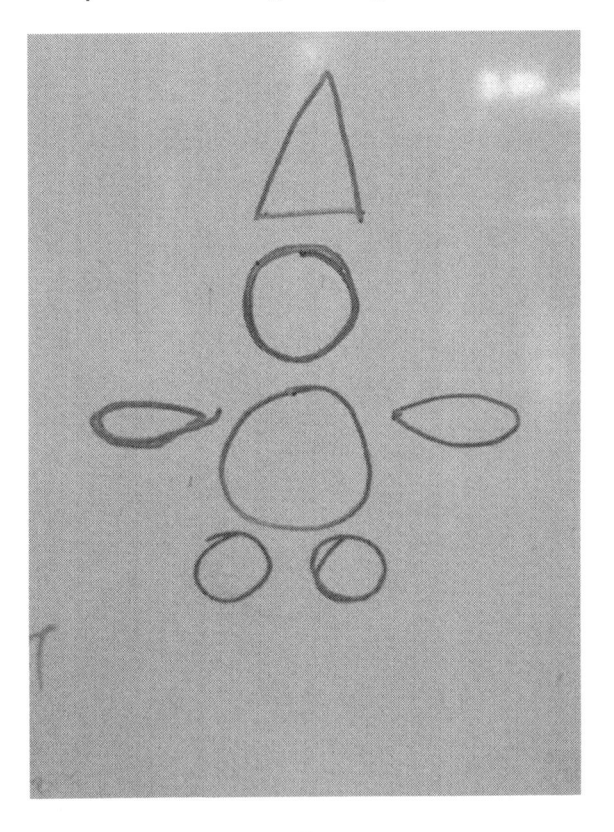

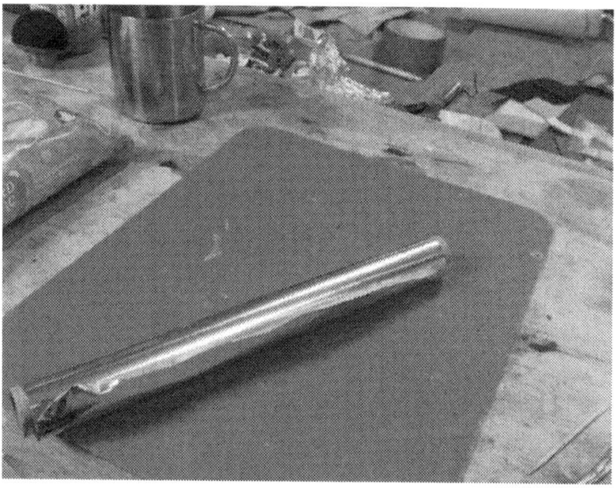

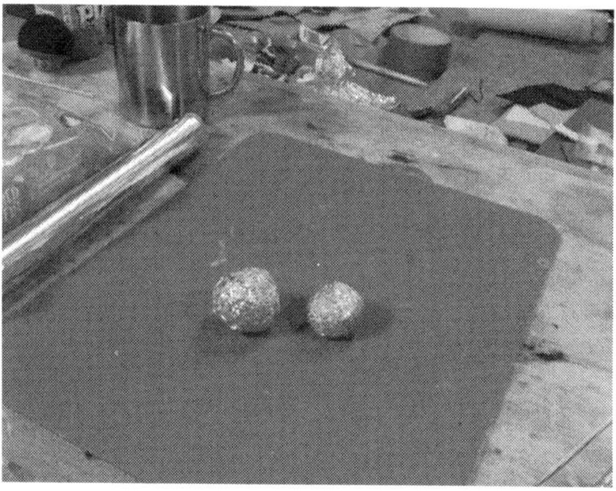

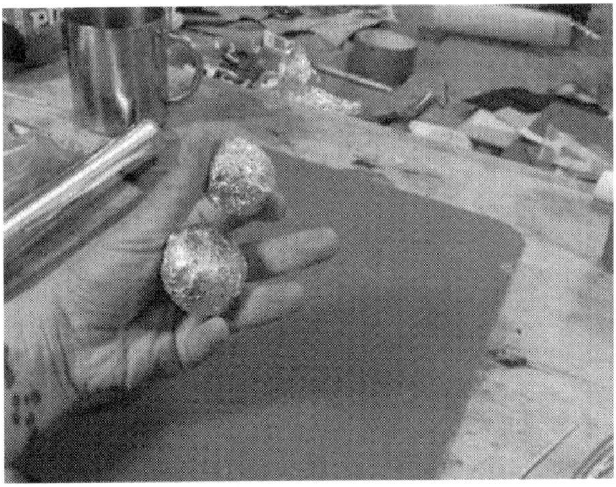

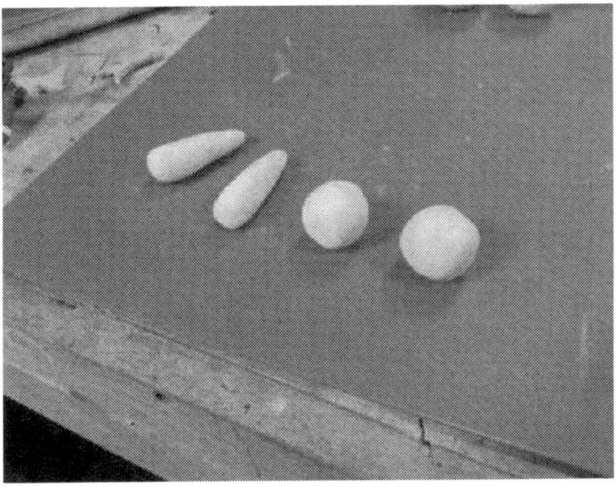

Our Gnome will be composed of seven pieces: the head, the

body, the arms twice, the legs twice, and, of course, the hat.

Both the head and the body

To begin, form two balls of tin foil, one approximately the size of a walnut and the other somewhat larger (think kinda like when you are building a snowman)

Make a flat piece of clay and wrap it over the two tin foil balls to protect them.

The legs are a pair of legs.

As a temporary solution, just roll two firm balls of clay that are somewhat smaller than the skull. There is no need for tinfoil.

The forearms

Roll out two long tear drop forms, varying the length according to your preference.

The hat is a nice touch.

create a cone out of the material

Step 2: Getting a Hold of Yourself...

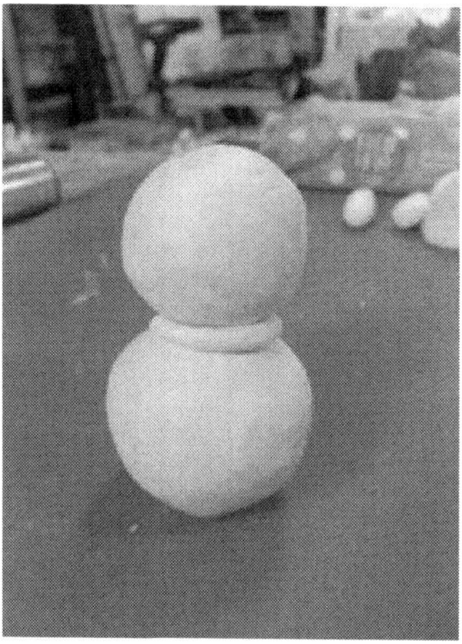

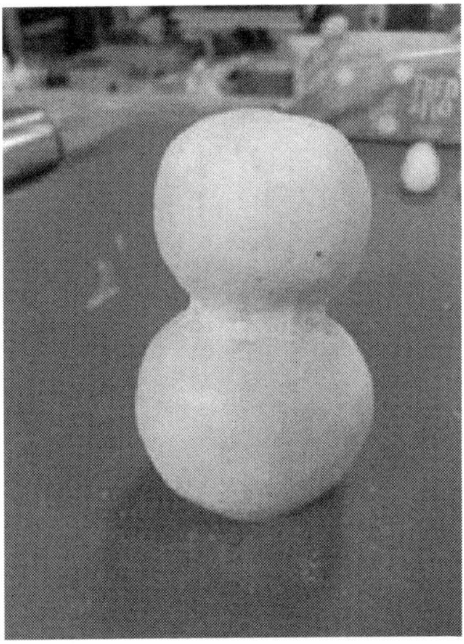

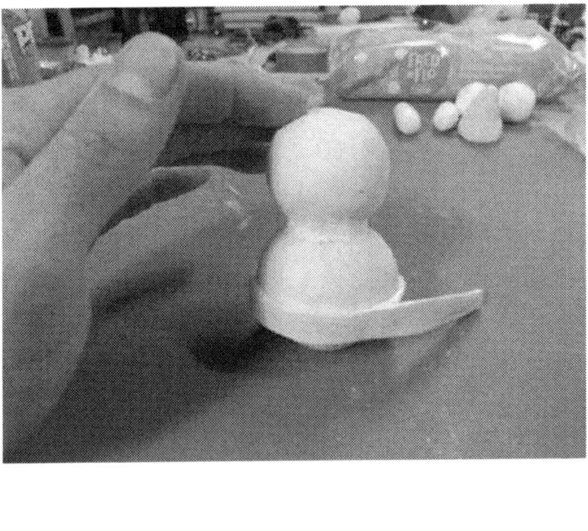

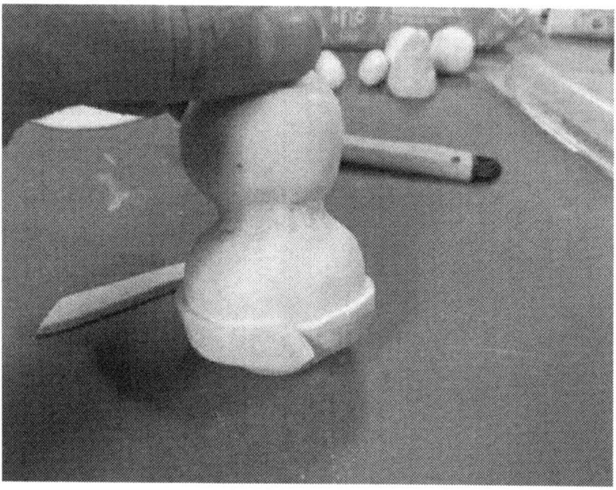

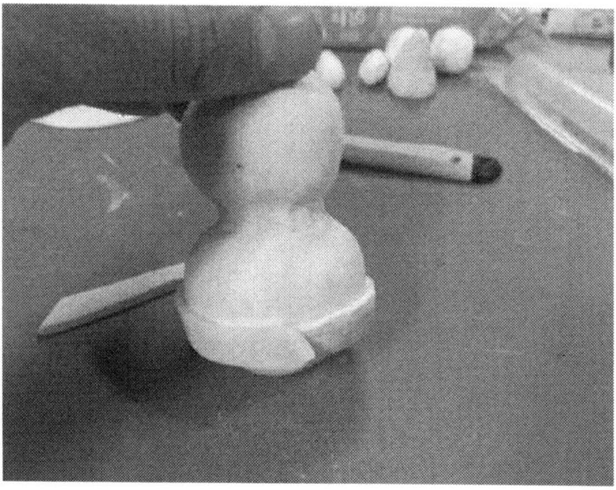

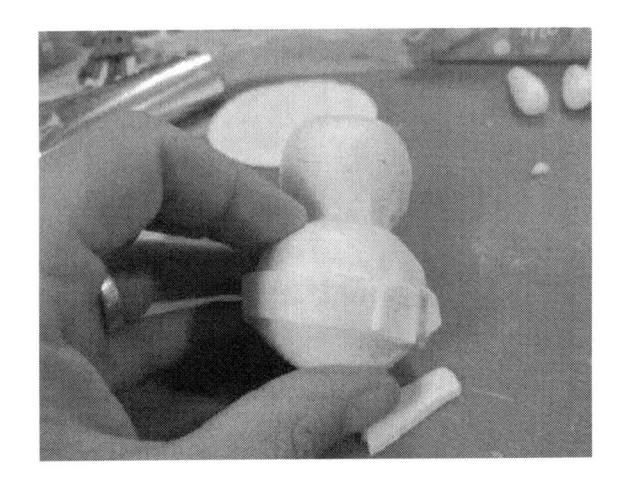

Assemble the head sphere onto the body, and roll out a thin snake of clay long enough to wrap around the point where your head sphere and the body come together. Smooth it into position after you've done so.

The belt is the next thing we'll be working on (we do this now so that the beard wont get in the way later)

Flatten out a long, thick snake that has been rolled out before. It's possible that you'll want to trim the side to keep it looking nice.

Begin by attaching one end of the clay to the front of your gnome's belly (about where you believe the belly button would be), and then wrapping it around his entire body.

Once it has been wrapped around the whole circumference, allow it to overhang slightly before trimming the excess into a point.

A square should be attached to the overlap in the same way a belt buckle would be attached.

Part 2 of Step 3: Getting a Head Start

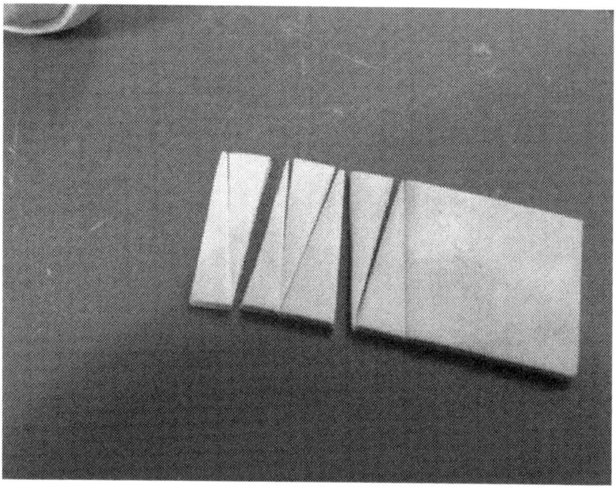

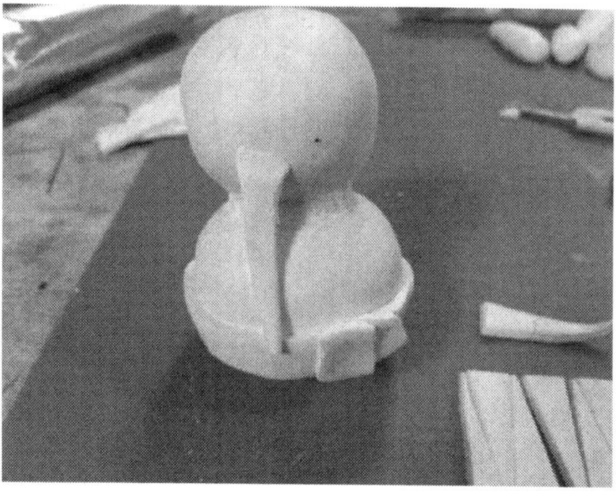

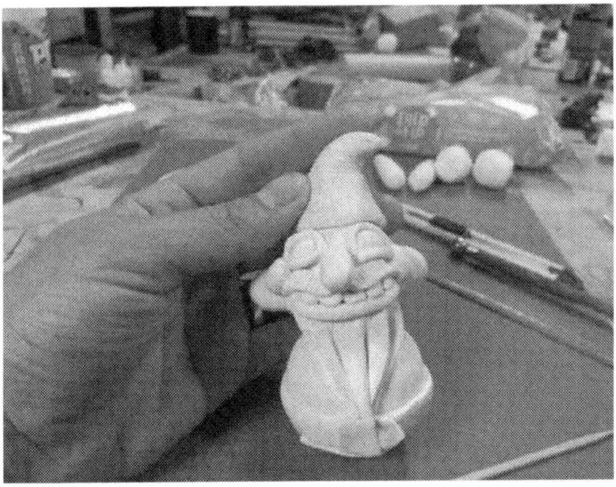

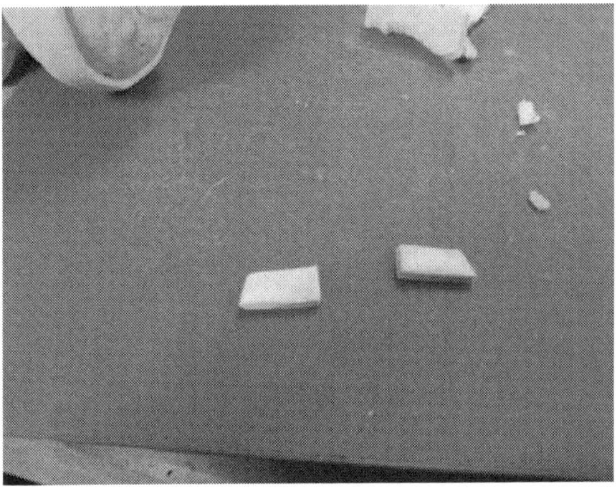

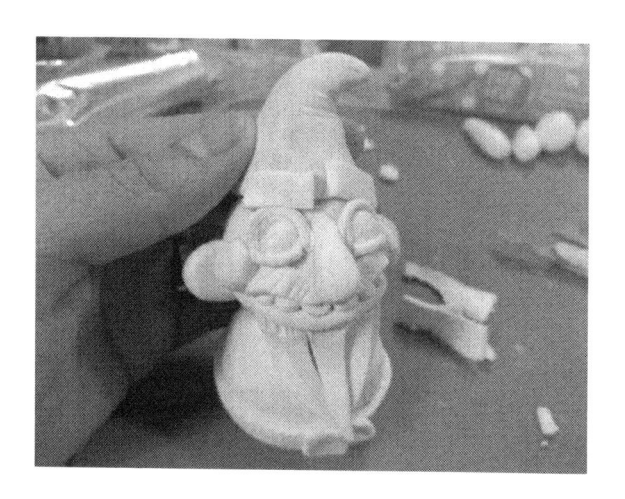

There appear to be a lot of stages in this section, but they are all extremely basic, so don't be concerned.

We're going to start with the beard and work our way up from there.

It has a beard.

Roll out a flat piece of clay and cut it into a rectangle that is about the length you want the beard to be across the shorter length of the rectangle, with the longer length of the rectangle being the shorter length of the rectangle (I hope that make sense)

Cut the rectangle into long triangles using a sharp knife. It is possible to obtain more clay out of your clay if you alternate the "base" of the triangle when cutting it.

Make many of them and connect the lengths of the beard along the "chin," starting from outside and working your way in. Make sure they are all securely secured.

The lower lip is the most prominent feature of the face.

Using your hands, roll out a snake of clay and place it to the area where the beard joins to the chin, moulding it into a grin or whatever mouth shape you like (who says it needs to be a happy gnome)

Dentures are the teeth.

Simply cut out several teeth shapes (squares, rounded, pointy?!?) and put them to the lower lip, slightly overhanging the bottom lip.

The Moustache is a must-have accessory.

Take a few little rectangles, each one approximately half the length of your gnome's mouth, shape them a little, and attach them to his mouth so that they just just overlap the teeth.

The Nose is the most important part of the body.

Attached in a teardrop form, slightly overhanging the moustache.

The eyes and the eyelids are a part of the face.

The eyes are made by rolling out a little ball and cutting it in half, then placing them on either side of the nose.

Make four tiny snakes to use as eyelids for the eyes. One should be placed below the eye and the points at the end should be blended in. One over the top of the eye and one over the bottom of the eye (if you overlap the lower lid a bit it looks a bit more realistic)

The cheeks and the ears.

Although the ears are nearly identical to the eyes, it may be necessary to flatten them somewhat before connecting them. When attaching the ears, make sure the edges are smoothed in.

The hat is a nice touch.

Construct the base of your cone such that it sits on your gnome's head rather than "floating" over it by slightly concaving the bottom. You may also sculpt wrinkles into the clay to give it a more cloth-like appearance, as well as bend the point of the clay a little (personal choice, you dont need to)

It is the brows that are important.

In the same way as you did with the moustache, but above the eyes Incorporating an overlap onto the hat gives it a more cartoony appearance. (See image below.)

Step four: Put your best foot forward.

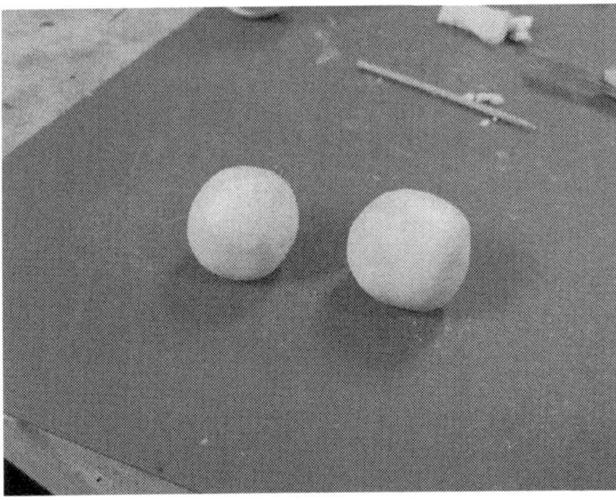

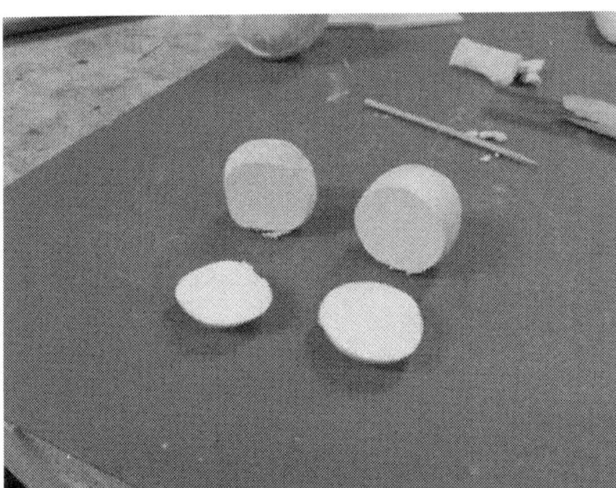

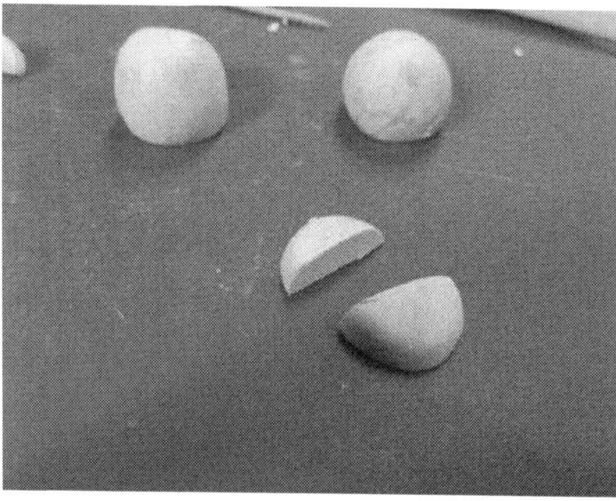

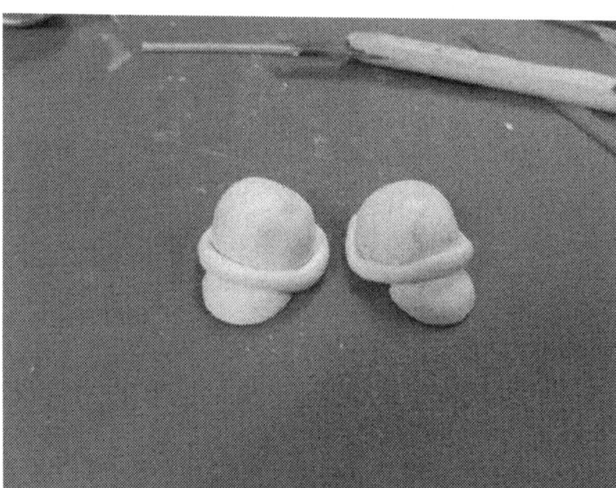

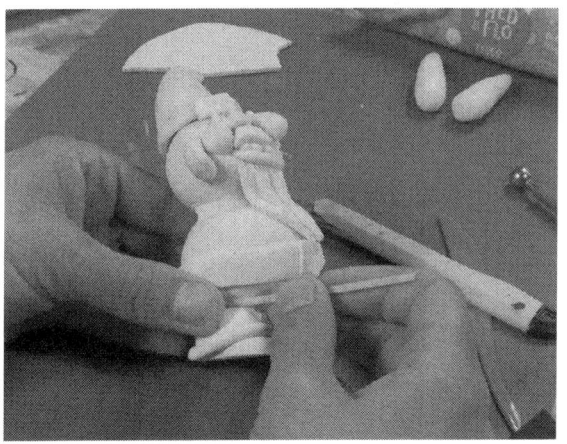

Take the two leg balls that we rolled before and cut the ends off of them using a sharp knife.

Only enough to provide a flat "base" for it.

Take one of the pieces you've cut off, halve it, and then tie it to the legs like shoes, like you would a shoelace.

Make two long snakes that are long enough to wrap around the base of the gnomes' legs and over their shoes, then wrap them around them (so it looks like trousers)

Attach them to the body, causing sores to be made to smooth the edges in (if needed you can do the same thing you did for the head and body)

Step 5: Raise Your Arms

We're almost there.

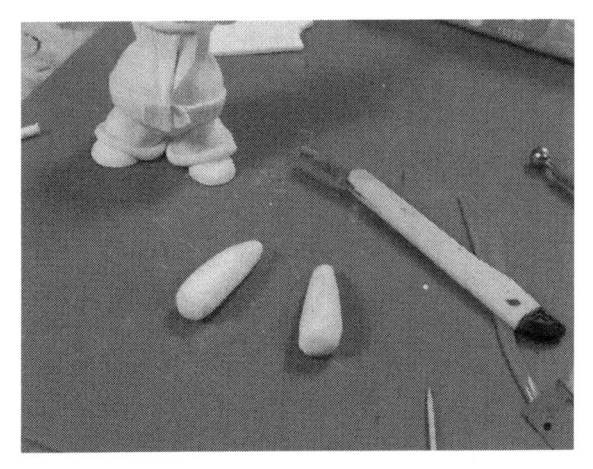

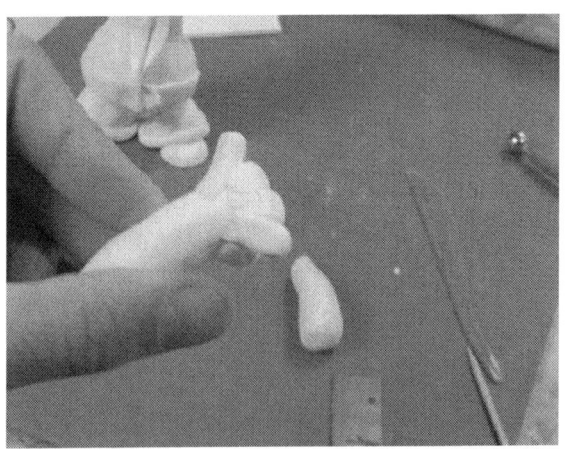

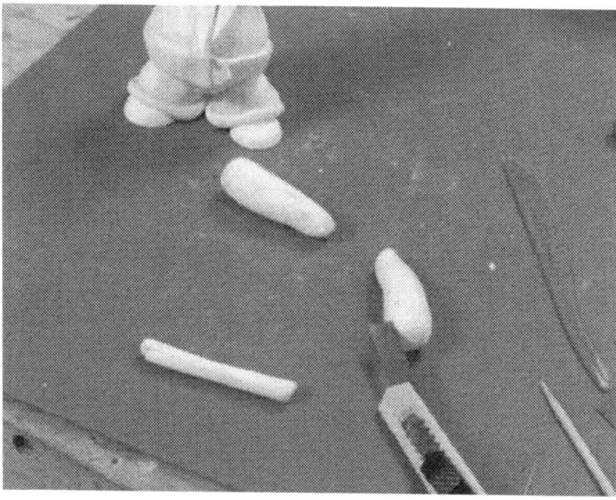

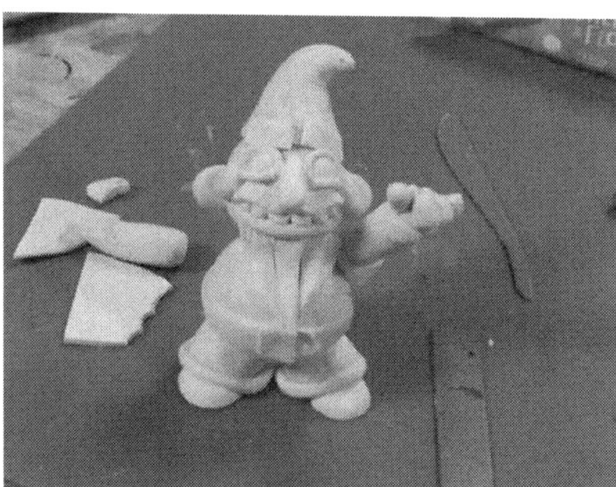

For the arms, we want to use our lengthy tear drop forms as a starting point.

To make the fingers, roll out a snake that is thick enough to be used as fingers and cut 10 pieces that are long enough to be used as fingers (you will need to use your judgement here again because everyone's arms will be a little different).

Begin connecting them to the larger end of the tear drop along one edge (not the centre), smoothing the ends in and bending the fingers into the correct position as necessary.

I then added little lumps to represent the knuckles and a

slightly larger lump to represent the elbow.

Once you have rolled/cut out a rectangle large enough to serve as the "shoulder" of your gnomes arm, wrap it over the "shoulder" and shape it to appear like the "sleeve" of his/her arm.

Attach the arms in the position you wish.

You might wish to add some finishing touches and embellishments at this point.

It is now ready to be baked according to the manufacturer's directions for your polymer clay.

Step 6: Add a Little Color to It

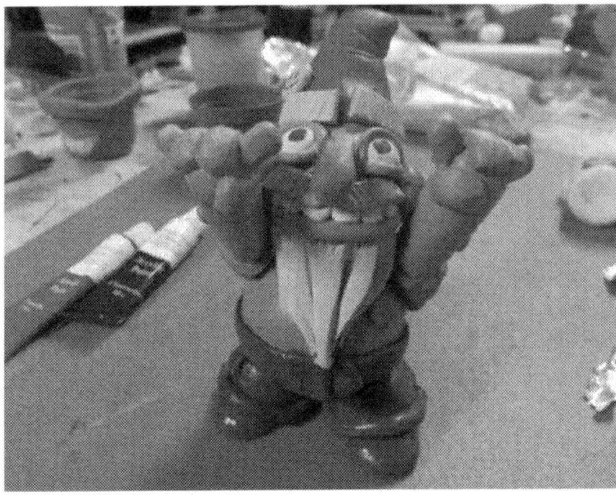

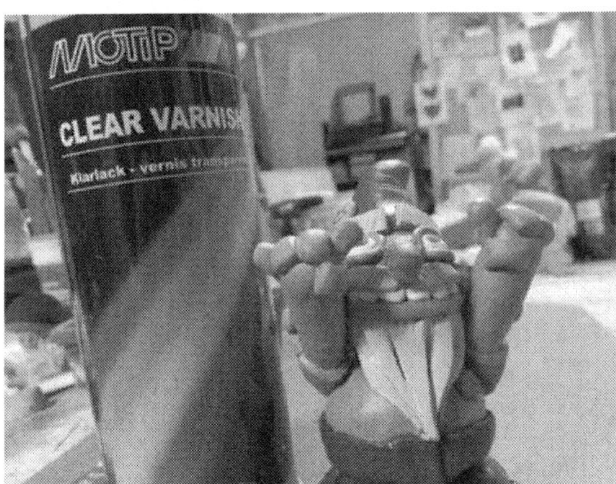
CLEAR VARNISH

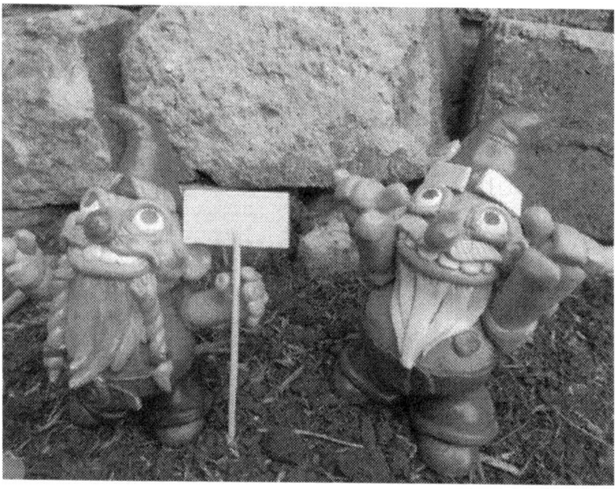

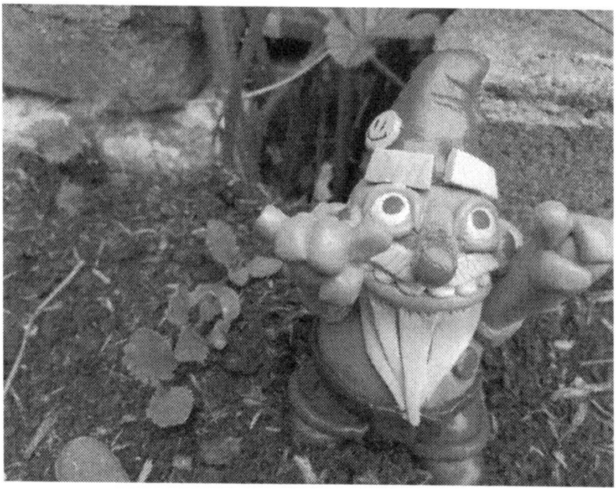

If you haven't already, let it cool completely before painting it. I don't believe you'll need a step-by-step guide here:)

After the paint has dried, apply a coat of varnish to protect it (mainly if you are going to have them outside)

And with that, we're done!!!

You've created a gnome, congratulations! Your gnome army's very first soldier, maybe.

As always, I hope you enjoyed this guide, and as always, I welcome your views, comments, and even images of your own Gnomes, which you can post in the comments area at the bottom of this article.

Good luck with your sculpting!

CHAPTER 4

HOW TO CARVE GNOMES WITH WOOD

Learn how to construct a gnome figure out of wood. It's a really basic chore, and for the most part, I just wanted to show off my gnome to everyone else.

Step 1: Obtaining Wood Salvage

When beginning off with whittling, it is important to choose the right wood. Many have abandoned up after selecting a piece of wood that proved to be intractable; yet, a flexible wood type vital to a positive first-time experience can be found. During my ninth-grade English class, I attempted a do-it-yourself whittling assignment, but I failed miserably and ended up demonstrating the rest of the class how to put together a skateboard instead. It was an awful piece of rubbish.

As a result, a 15-year plan is already in motion. My thoughts were constantly racing, so as I was out jogging one weekend, I noticed broken wood barriers from several automobile accidents and pondered whether they were made of a delicate hardwood like rosewood. I selected a piece and brought it home with me.

As I investigated it, I discovered that it had been infested with termites, so I treated the wood with some termite spray that I had on hand. After allowing it to cure for a day, I cleansed it well with soap. It had been completed.

(There are some nice parts that I'm considering rescuing and transforming into totem poles.)

Step 2: Making a mark and cutting it out

Take out your jigsaw and clamp the wood in your vise-grip, and start cutting. You don't want to waste time callousing your hands with a block. After the initial cut, draw a rough outline of the object using a pencil. The image below is really a digital representation of the project because I began it before debating whether or not to share it.

Step 3: Callousing with a Xacto Knife

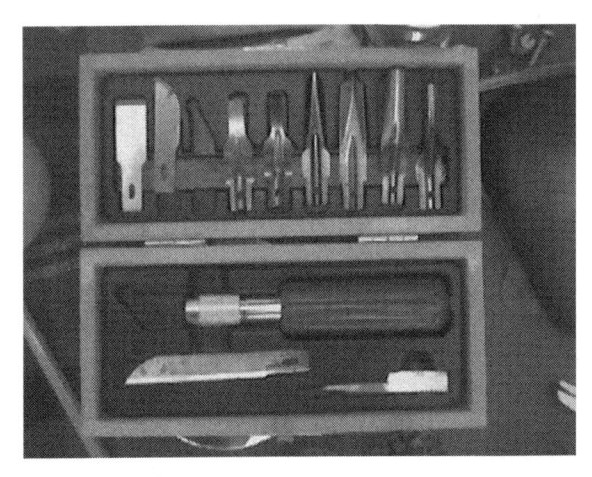

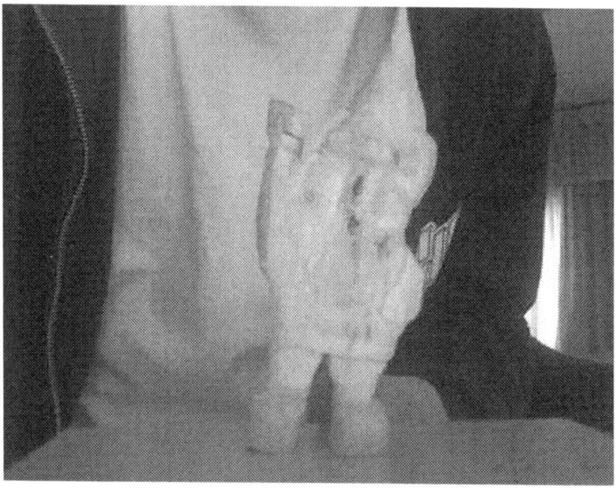

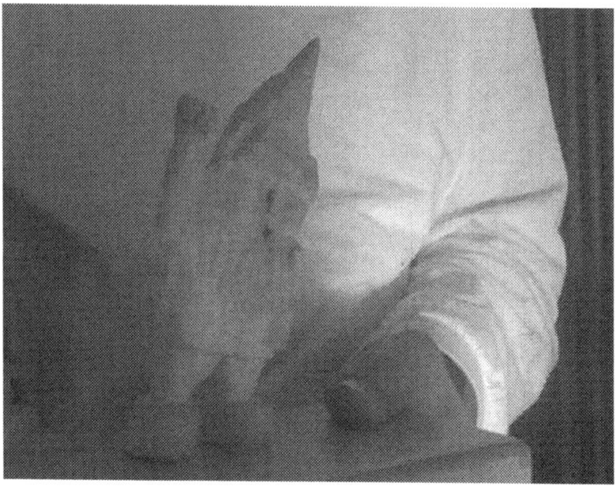

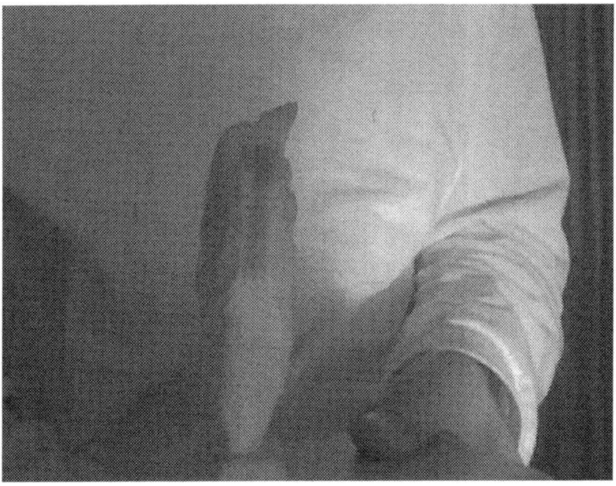

Consequently, the greatest blade to begin with is really the long blade, which is, in my opinion, the ideal whiting tool. It only makes sense when you use long strokes.

Continue to sketch your shapes and features until you get something that looks like this.

Step 4: Paint Your Wooden Structure

I used acrylic base paints that I blended together to achieve the appropriate hues. I really used several different coats of paint and switched up the colors until I was satisfied with the result.

Anyway, this is simple material, but it may serve as an inspiration to someone.

THE END

Printed in Great Britain
by Amazon